IT'S SCIENCE!

Light and dark

IT'S SCIENCE!

Light and dark

Sally Hewitt

W

FRANKLIN WATTS

LONDON•SYDNEY

First published in 1998 by Franklin Watts
96 Leonard Street, London EC2A 4XD
Paperback edition 2000

Franklin Watts Australia
14 Mars Road
Lane Cove
NSW 2066

Series editor: Rachel Cooke
Designer: Mo Choy
Picture research: Susan Mennell
Photography: Ray Moller unless otherwise acknowledged
Consultant: Sally Nankivell-Aston

A CIP catalogue record for this book
is available from the British Library.

ISBN 0 7496 2903 7 (hbk); 0 7496 3768 4 (pbk)

Dewey Classification 531

Printed in Malaysia

Acknowledgements:
Bruce Coleman pp. 9br (Alain Compost), 11bl (Kevin Rushby), 11br (Charles and Sandra Hood),
12t (Felix Labhardt), 27tl (Kim Taylor), 27tr (M. Fogden), 27bl (M. Fogden);
Robert Harding pp. 17t (Mark Stephenson) 24t (J.M. Francillon);
Image Bank pp. 7 (Alain Choisnet), 10t (Max Dannenbaum), 10b (F. D'Elbee), 20tl (Joseph van Os);
Oxford Scientific Films p. 20tr (Harold Taylor); Tony Stone Images p.17br (Terry Vine).
Thank you to Tridias, 6 Bennett Street, Bath BA1 2QP, 01225 314730 for their help with the
objects photographed for this book on pp. 14, 19 and 26.
Thanks as well to our models: Miles Wong-Tester, James Moller,
Nakita Ogugua, Luke Richardson and Charlotte Harrison.

Contents

Light and dark   6

Daylight   8

Darkness   10

Casting shadows   12

Seeing   14

Reflection   16

Shining through   18

Bigger and smaller   20

Snapshots   22

Rainbows   24

A colourful world   26

Useful words   28

Index   30

About this book   30

Light and dark

In the **daytime**, the **sun** lights up the **earth** and we can see what is happening all around us.

At night when the sun goes down, the earth becomes dark. We have to find ways of lighting up the dark so that we can see.

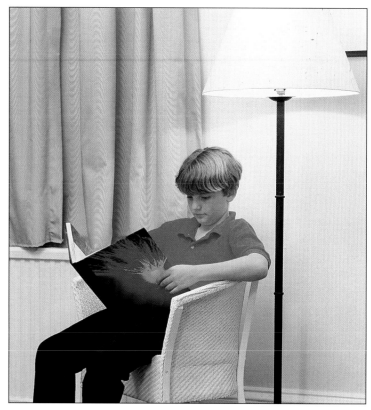

💡 THINK ABOUT IT!

Do you play games or read during dark evenings?
What could you do in the evening if you couldn't light up the dark?

Street lights and car head-lights help to light up the dark.

What other ways can you think of to do this?

TRY IT OUT!

At **night-time**, close the curtains and turn out the light in your bedroom. Is there any light getting in? What can you see?

Turn on the light. What can you see now?

Daylight

The sun is a gigantic
ball of hot, burning gas.
The earth is a ball of rock,
much smaller than the sun.
The sun is a long way from
our planet earth, but it gives
us heat and light.

Each day the earth turns round.
During the day, the part of earth
we live on faces the sun.
At night, it faces away.

 TRY IT OUT!

Pretend a ball is the earth.
Make a drawing of yourself, cut it out
and stick it on the ball. Hold the ball up
in the sun, so that one side is brightly lit.
Turn the ball round gradually – watch
yourself move from daytime into night.

The sun is up and it is daytime.
What are the people who use these
things doing today?
What do you do during the day?

 THINK ABOUT IT!

Why do you think most people and animals are
awake in the day and asleep at night? Can you
think of any animals that are awake at night?

9

Darkness

At night we can see the **moon** shining in the sky.

The moon is a dark, cold ball of rock, like the earth.
The sun shines on it and makes it look bright.

 THINK ABOUT IT!

On a cloudy night, we cannot see any light from the moon.
It is very dark.
What happens to sunlight when it is a cloudy day?

When you shut your eyes, your eyelids keep the light out of your eyes. Shut your eyes. Can you see anything?

 TRY IT OUT!

Try making a very dark corner in your bedroom like this one, by keeping out as much light as you can.

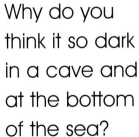 Why do you think it so dark in a cave and at the bottom of the sea?

 LOOK AGAIN

Look again at page 7.
How do we light up the dark?

11

Casting shadows

Can you see how light **rays** come from the sun in straight lines?

Rays of light cannot bend, go round corners or shine through a solid object like you!

 TRY IT OUT!

On a sunny day, stand with your back to the sun. Because the sun cannot shine through you, your body will cast a dark **shadow**. Move around and watch your shadow do the same things as you.

Light from a candle shines out all around it. Look at the shadows of the mugs falling in every direction.

A beam of torch light only shines where you point the torch. What has happened to the shadows of the mugs now?

TRY IT OUT!

Make a shadow puppet show. Cut out cardboard figures like these and tape them on to a stick. Shine a bright light on to a plain wall and hold the figures between them. Move them around and start your show!

13

Seeing

We see when light shines on to the things around us and into our open eyes.
We can see shapes and colours, and we can tell how far away things are.

Paul is walking to the table. What can
he see around him?

💡 THINK ABOUT IT!

How would Paul get safely to the table if he had his eyes shut?
Why would it be much harder?

The coloured circle in your eye is the **iris**. The black circle, called the **pupil**, is a hole in the iris. You see when light shines through your pupils into your eye.

The iris can make the pupil bigger to let in more light. It can make the pupil smaller to keep light out.

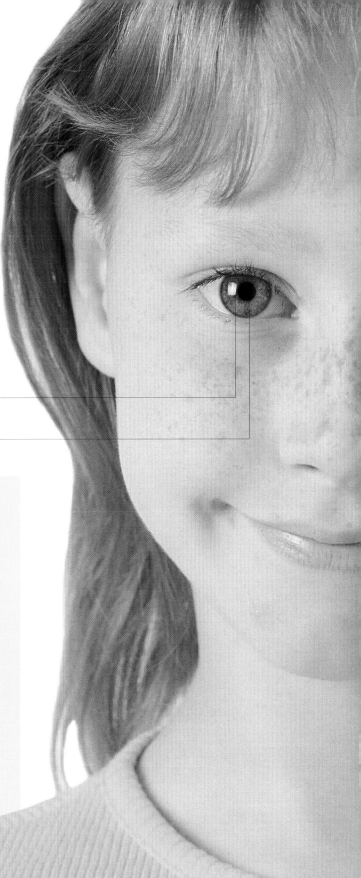

pupil

iris

 TRY IT OUT!

Look out of the window on a sunny day or into a brightly lit room. Now look at your pupils in a mirror. Note what size they are.

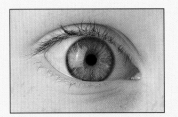 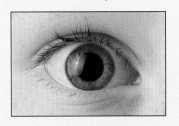

Look into a dark place for a few moments. Look at your pupils: are they bigger or smaller? They will probably have opened up to let in as much light as possible.

Reflection

When you look into a mirror, you can see your **reflection**.

 TRY IT OUT!

Collect some objects like the ones on this page. Look at them and feel them.

Do they look dull or shiny?
Do they feel rough or smooth?
Can you see your reflection when you look at them?
Which one is the flattest, shiniest object?
Which one shows you the clearest reflection of your face?

THINK ABOUT IT!

Write your name and look at its reflection in a mirror. What is different about the reflection? Does the same thing happen with your reflection?

You can see clear reflections in smooth, flat water.

Wind ripples the water and spoils the reflections.

 TRY IT OUT!

Find a puddle after it has rained and the sun is shining. Can you see a clear reflection of yourself in the puddle? Ripple the puddle with your hand. What happens to your reflection now?

Shining through

Different things happen to light when it shines on to a book, a window and a net curtain because they are all made of different materials.

A book is **opaque**. You cannot see through it and light cannot shine through it.

Glass is **transparent**. You can see through it and light shines through it.

This net curtain is **translucent**. It lets some light shine though.

👁 LOOK AGAIN

Look again at page 12 to find something opaque, and at page 10 to find something translucent.

All these things are made of different materials.

TRY IT OUT!

Make a collection of things like the ones in the picture.

Hold each one up to the light. Which ones can you see through?

Shine a torch on to them. Which ones does the light shine through?
Which ones cast a shadow?

Separate them into groups of opaque objects, transparent objects
and translucent objects.

Bigger and smaller

A **lens** is a curved piece of transparent material such as glass or plastic. Lenses can make things look bigger or smaller, nearer or further away.

There are lenses in **binoculars**, a **microscope** and a **magnifying glass**.

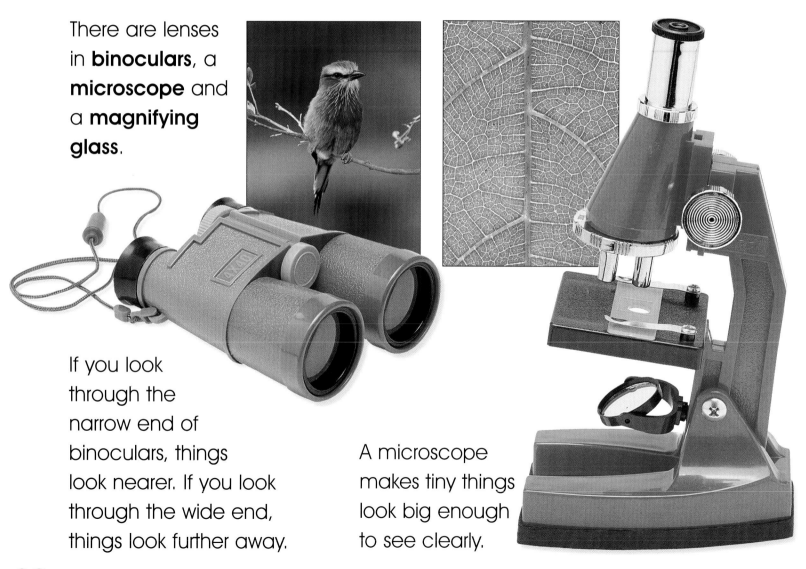

If you look through the narrow end of binoculars, things look nearer. If you look through the wide end, things look further away.

A microscope makes tiny things look big enough to see clearly.

A magnifying glass makes small things look bigger.

 TRY IT OUT!

Make a collection of small things and
look at them through a magnifying glass.
Look at your skin, nails and hair as well.

Special lenses inside our eyes let us see things sharply. Some people's
eye-lenses do not work properly so they have to wear glasses or
contact lenses.

Glasses have lenses inside
them which help people to
see more clearly.
Contact lenses work in
the same way but
they are put straight
on to the eye.

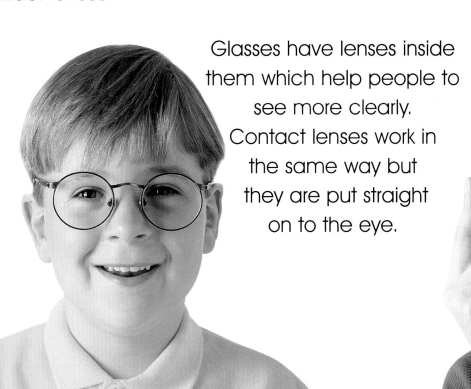

Snapshots

Photographs
are easy
to take.
First, load
a film into
a camera.

Next, look through the eyepiece to find the
picture you want and press the shutter button.
A shutter blinks open to let light in through
the camera lens on to the film.
This takes the photograph.

Have the film
developed to
get a print of the
photograph you took.

 LOOK AGAIN

Look again at page 15 to
find how light reaches the
lenses in your eyes.

A moving film is made by taking a series of still pictures like these very quickly with a special movie camera.

The pictures are shone on to a screen one after the other so quickly that you see the person running along.

TRY IT OUT!

Fold a piece of thin white paper in half.
Copy the sleepy face onto the bottom half of the paper.
Trace the face onto the top half but add open eyes.
Pull the bottom corner up and down very fast – watch the eyes open and shut!

Rainbows

We call light from the sun white light because it looks white.

When it is raining and sunlight shines through raindrops, the white light is split into the seven different colours of the **rainbow**: violet, dark blue, light blue, green, yellow, orange and red.

 TRY IT OUT!

Blow some bubbles in the sunlight.
Can you see rainbows in the bubbles?

24

The colours of the rainbow can be mixed together to make white!

 TRY IT OUT!

You will need:
– white card
– tracing paper
– felt tip pens the colours
  of the rainbow
– a pencil
– scissors.

Trace this circle on to the white card.

Colour in the segments.
Make the colours as bright as you can.

Cut out the circle and carefully push the pencil through the centre.

Spin the card and watch the colours of the rainbow turn white.

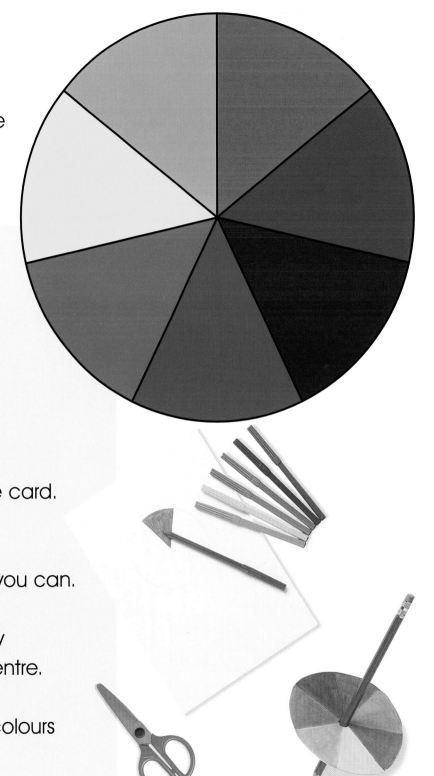

A colourful world

The world is a colourful place. Can you see
all the colours of the rainbow in this picture?
What other colours can you see?

 THINK ABOUT IT!

Imagine what the world would be
like if there were no colours and
everything was black and white!

Animals, plants and insects use colour in all kinds of different ways.

Insects are attracted by colourful flowers. The bright colours tell them that they will find something good to eat.

It is difficult to see a green snake hiding amongst the leaves.

The bright yellow and black stripes of this frog warn hungry animals that it is poisonous to eat.

 LOOK AGAIN

Look again through this book. What blue things can you find, what red things and what yellow things?

Useful words

Binoculars You look through a pair of binoculars with both eyes to see things that are too far away to see clearly with your eyes on their own. Binoculars make things look nearer.

Daytime Daytime begins when the sun rises in the morning and ends when the sun sets in the evening. It is light during daytime.

Earth Earth is where we live. It is a large ball of rock called a planet. The earth gets its heat and light from the sun, which it slowly moves around. The earth turns round once each day.

Iris The iris is the coloured part of your eye. It has a black hole in its centre, the pupil (see page 29). The iris controls the size of the pupil.

Lens A lens is a curved piece of see-through or tranparent material. Depending on its shape, a lens makes things look bigger or smaller.

Magnifying glass When you look at small things through a magnifying glass, they look bigger.

Microscope You look through a microscope to see things that are too small to see clearly with just your eyes. It makes them look much, much bigger.

Moon The moon is a ball or rock that moves around the earth. Nothing lives on the moon. We can only see it when it is lit up by the sun.

Night-time Night-time begins when the sun sets in the evening and ends when the sun rises in the morning. It is dark during night-time.

Opaque Something is opaque if light cannot shine through it.

Photograph A photograph is a print of a picture taken by a camera. Light goes through the camera lens on to a film, which is changed by the light.

Pupil The pupil is the part of the eye that looks black. It is really a hole that light can shine through.

Rainbow A rainbow is the bow-shaped arc formed when sunlight shines through raindrops and splits into seven different colours.

Ray Light travels in straight lines. We call these straight lines rays or beams.

Reflection You see your reflection when light rays bounce, or reflect, off a shiny surface like a mirror. The picture you see is the wrong way round.

Shadow A shadow is a patch of darkness made when light cannot shine through a solid object like you.

Sun The huge ball of burning gases that gives heat and light to the earth.

Translucent Something is translucent if only some light can shine through it.

Transparent Something is transparent when all light can shine through it.

Index

binoculars 20, 28
camera 22. 23
colour 14, 24, 25, 26, 27
dark 6, 7, 10, 11, 12, 15
daytime 6, 8, 9, 28
earth 6, 8, 10, 28
eyes 11, 14, 15, 21, 28, 29
iris 15, 28
lens 20, 21, 22, 28
light 6, 7, 8, 11, 12, 13, 14, 15, 18,
  19, 24, 28, 29
magnifying glass 20, 21, 28
materials 18, 19
microscope 20, 28
moon 10, 28
moving pictures 23
night-time 6, 7, 8, 9, 10, 29
opaque 18, 19, 29
photograph 22, 29
pupil 15, 29
rainbow 24, 25, 26, 29
ray 12, 29
reflection 16, 17, 29
seeing 6, 7, 10, 14, 15, 18, 19, 20, 21
shadow 12, 13, 19, 29
sun 6, 8, 9, 10, 17, 24. 29
translucent 18, 19, 29
transparent 18, 19, 20, 29

About this book

Children are natural scientists. They learn by touching and feeling, noticing, asking questions and trying things out for themselves. The books in the *It's Science!* series are designed for the way children learn. Familiar objects are used as starting points for further learning. *Light and dark* starts with daylight and explores light and colour.

Each double page spread introduces a new topic, such as reflection. Information is given, questions asked and activities suggested that encourage children to make discoveries and develop new ideas for themselves.
Look out for these panels throughout the book:

TRY IT OUT! indicates a simple activity, using safe materials, that proves or explores a point.
THINK ABOUT IT! indicates a question inspired by the information on the page but which points the reader to areas not covered by the book.
LOOK AGAIN introduces a cross-referencing activity which links themes and facts through the book.

Encourage children not to take the familiar world for granted. Point things out, ask questions and enjoy making scientific discoveries together.